# Pills, Pearls, and Potions

by Dr. Jane A. Passamonte

> Dedicated to Beth and Gregory Robinson
> for their faithful and tireless efforts.

## PREFACE

These poems and articles are the residue of dealing and befriending in casual conversation over many years as a pharmacist, family medical doctor, and always willing to lend an ear to friends and strangers.

Given an opportunity, it would not be the ache or broken bone or new baby - it would be the loneliness within them - or the misunderstanding from these people needed a dose to lift their spirits - a moment to hope the unreal - to have someone listen to them with an attentive ear - a warm smile - and a touch of human understanding - to let that spark of sincerity and love reach into their hearts.

A poem is the essence of true literature - a dose of a long story that lifts the spirits within.

© Copyright 1997 Dr. Jane A. Passamonte

Second Edition, First Printing
February 1997

ISBN 1-884441-02-5

For information, contact:
B&G Supply Co., Inc.
P.O. Box 130092
Tyler, Texas 75713

Design, Typography, & Printing by

Tyler Press
div. of Starboard Enterprises, Inc.
Tyler, Texas

Pills, Pearls, and Potions — by Dr. Jane A. Passamonte

## UNDERSTANDING

Understanding is the bridge to the hearts of our fellowmen.

Wars are fought when words fail and there is no understanding.

Friends have become enemies cause words and accusations are flung at each other - and when they ran out of words — violence of thought or action was used - and friendships broken for lack of understanding.

But to have understanding you must first have some wisdom. You must be able to see - and reason - and think. You must ask yourself — Why — When — Where — What — Who — Which.

For understanding you need patience. We see and understand different - at other times and places - at other days. Understanding is getting help from others who can enlighten us - from friends and family and from Divine sources. Understanding is the pathway to peace and serenity - to a fullness of living, to a joyness in being. Understanding makes it possible to reach out a helping hand to a friend or foe - young or old - because with understanding comes a built-in smile - a warm heart and an eager spirit.

Pills, Pearls, and Potions — by Dr. Jane A. Passamonte

## WORLD OF WOES

Come my child - born of pain and tears.
Into a world of wars and woes,
Come into the sunshine and the trees.
They are there for you and me-
As well as the wind and the rain-
And the flowers that scent the breeze.
The setting sun opens the gate to a sky,
Studded with jewelled stars and a burnished moon.
They are all free for you and me.
Let those who risk to wreck the lives
For greed or gold - for reasons sad and old,
Drown in their pit of guilt.
While you and I climb the mount of desire,
We will cling to the top - one rock at a time-
And reach for a star - the jewel of delight,
That fills the soul with the spark of divinity.

Pills, Pearls, and Potions — by Dr. Jane A. Passamonte

## THE VOID IN THE HEART

I saw Grandma on a sunny day...
Staring out the window while rocking away.
A subtle smile... and stars in her eyes...
Bejewelled her face.
Beyond an old apple tree... a verdant valley...
Cast their spell... quietly... she rocked.
"Grandma"... I asked as I sat beside her...
"May I share some of your memories?"
My child... the sun and the rain...
The storms and the rainbows.

Soon came school and friends galore
But Albert was special... soon held my hand...
We walked the fields... ran up the hills...
The years passed... we found a bond...
And in each other we saw ourselves as one.
With marriage came Ellen... and soon the war.
Ellen was two years... and Albert was Captain.
One day a notice... Captain Albert was lost at sea.
Each restless night... each lonely day...
Each dream of waves... each hope would fade.
Each tear would flow in the wind.
To my Albert out in the sea.
Ellen grew and filled the void... my soul with love and joy.
Then I welcomed Robert... Ellen's dream.
A handsome man... and deepdown... I felt the touch of Albert.

Pills, Pearls, and Potions         by Dr. Jane A. Passamonte

A spark lighted my heart and soul and
Lighted the dark caverns of my mind.
I would talk to Albert... and hum his favorite tunes...
And waited for Robert to fill the emptiness in my soul.
Soon came you... and completed the emptiness in my soul.
I sing to Albert... I laugh with Robert...
And you my Grandson...

Are the sparks that light my life.

Pills, Pearls, and Potions     by Dr. Jane A. Passamonte

## OH YOUTH

Youth is when you think you know everything, yet daily you learn something new.
When your wishes and dreams are beyond your means
Yet you reach for them with laughter and screams.
A handful of stars seems not so far
And the moon is a long way off.
Your friends are forever
You have nothing to lose.
The days are not long enough
The dawns come too soon.
Parents do not understand. How could they.
Their minds are cluttered with facts and learning, experience and yearning.
At 30 and 40, or maybe 50 and 60
They are much too serious.
The stars are much farther, the dreams more real.
Their wishes far reaching for the youth in their care.
They too were young some time ago
They too reached for the stars
And dreamed and laughed.
They danced in the rain and sang in the wind.
But now they are content to look back with a smile and a tear
That all of you may find your way
And walk on the footprints and trail they left for you
Yes, just for you
And share with you their treasure of youth, and ultimate Love.

Pills, Pearls, and Potions — by Dr. Jane A. Passamonte

## YOUR INNER SECRET

There is much that you and I can do, my friend, to find peace and happiness and days of smiles and nights of restful sleep. There is an old Irish jingle that says, " 'Tis a secret untold to hearts cruel and cold. Tho 'tis sung by the angels above." Look into yourself and count the good things you have done for others. Have you been honest to yourself and others... have you given of yourself to make others happy, or touched someone in trouble to show you cared... have you held the hand of one in sorrow, or hugged a tearful one, or even a long lost friend... have you shared anything with a needy one, even to just show you cared, and have you been generous with your smiles and friendly handshakes? When you have seen yourself for what you are, light a candle and watching it, meditate. Look back on your yesterdays and yesteryears. That is your past. You and the candle are your present. Do not be frightened of its fragility. You have braved the vast fields of your past. You see its victories and defeats, the ecstasies and the tears. You have come a long way. You can grade yourself and plan for a new tomorrow. You and the candle. You will have more wisdom and courage now that you know yourself. You and I and the candle are still fragile, but we must carry on, play our part, build better castles for our souls, and reach out. For as the candle gives us light and hope, so we give to others and fulfill our dreams in the smiles of our fellowmen and women. Yes, tomorrow is yours and mine. We must not fail, for we are part of the whole. We must reach out and hold tight the fragile light of the candle of hope, and the hand of friendship.

Pills, Pearls, and Potions — by Dr. Jane A. Passamonte

## OH IGNORANCE

Oh, Ignorance, cast thy bliss into the deepest sea.
And tell thy comrade Greed
"The best of Treasures are free
They are there for you and me."

## TREASURES

To hold a daisy in your palm
And squash the sea from waveswept sand.
To watch a feather in the breeze
And sense the frailty of a candle's flame.
To view a fiery dawn, or a serene sunset.
To hear the call of the loon, or a baby laugh.
To drink from a gushing spring
Or climb a mountain trail.
These treasures abound
For you and me, and all are free.

Pills, Pearls, and Potions — by Dr. Jane A. Passamonte

## THE MYTH OF YOUTH

Ah, youth, you are the promise of tomorrow.
And the reality of Today.
Long ago, like you, we reached for the stars,
And dreamed of victories.
We danced in the wind
And sang in the rain.

Youth is the hope of mankind.
Lift your voices
And dare to do great deeds
For youth, like the dawn
Comes on like thunder
And soon is gone.

## UNLOCK A WORLD OF SMILES

Man is ashamed to cry and afraid to laugh.  Holding critical emotions imprisoned in a stoic face and attitude merely leads to bursting the gentle and delicate threads that knit our emotions, fears, love, hate anxiety, anger.  Tears or laughter let out that inner pressure and save us from ourselves.  Let go the sordid Ego that stifles love and reason.  Reach out a hand of Friendship and unlock a world of Smiles.

Pills, Pearls, and Potions — by Dr. Jane A. Passamonte

## LOUISE

You and I my friend
And Mandy, too
Will travel the byway and trails.
We will climb the mountains
And cross the burning sands of the Planet Earth.
In search of love and peace and understanding.
It's a big and lonely Planet
With people like you and me.
We will sing a song
A song of happiness and love
To lift the spirit, to bring a smile
And leave the world a better place
Cause we were here.

Pills, Pearls, and Potions ——— by Dr. Jane A. Passamonte

## THE STARS ARE THE LIMIT

Life is a drama embellished by dream and fantasy and the splendor of color. What you think of yourself is far more important than what others think. What you aspire to and work for, like your life depended on it, is most important. For as Les Brown says, your life does depend on it. Reach as high as you can. The stars are for taking, the dreams are for you to harvest. Take charge of yourself. Do not blame others for your fears and trepidation. You are the captain of your boat on the sea of life. You must sail the storms and the calms. You must know your goal, your port of call. And you can reach it all. Just try and try again.

## THE STAR OF HOPE

Come, my friend, and shed your dreary thoughts.
Sweep the cobwebs from your reverie
And let the light of hope
Pierce the dark recesses of your mind.
For you and I, my friend, there is a star in the sky
To lead us on our way.

Pills, Pearls, and Potions — by Dr. Jane A. Passamonte

## THE THREAD THAT HOLDS

In dealing with each other if we must survive, deal with warmth and understanding. Otherwise, the delicate thread that holds us together soon breaks, and we will be condemned to wander aimlessly in a desert of frustration, emptiness and loneliness.

## PRAISE THE CONTENTS

Dear Amy,

Forget the painful remarks and taunts of people who judge others by their appearance. They also judge a package by its wrapping, not its contents. They are also living a shallow life of mind and body, and miss the true values of living.

Deep inside of you is a heart and soul and love of your fellowpersons, that may not be as well wrapped as the mass of people. The wrapping was issued to you at birth, you had no choice. But the contents are a gift from God, your parents and the whims of our environment.

One must not brag about or condemn the packaging, but we must be proud of the contents. Better to love and wish the best for your fellowmen. As to the critics, forgive their ignorance and misunderstanding. If they could find their full potential, if they could see their inner selves for what they are, their inner weaknesses, their misplaced values, and be grateful to their God and family for the many inner valuable assets, talents and blessings, then they would love others regardless of the wrappings. Remember, we do not belong to each other, we belong to God and learn to live with each other.

Pills, Pearls, and Potions — by Dr. Jane A. Passamonte

## THE GIFT OF YOURSELF

Life puts many of us through various ways of testing us for our journey in this world.  The test may be sickness, accident, drugs, hunger, loneliness, depression, etc.  Some fail the test and end up in jail, death, or invalidism.  The rest end up as outstanding characters, who, understanding life's meaning, accomplish a great deal and realize that happiness and fulfillment is measured not in money or materialism, or what they can take, but what they can give to others of themselves.

## YOU AND YOUR INNER SELF

Challenge yourself and test yourself to find and know your inner values, the truth about yourself.  Your strengths and weaknesses, your talents, your courage and your fears.  Then you will find peace and serenity and confidence.  You will know who you are and which way to go forward and share your inner gifts with others.

Pills, Pearls, and Potions ———————————————— by Dr. Jane A. Passamonte

## MARTHA

Too many tomorrows Martha
Are dead in the dust of yesterday.
No more moons, my dear.
Nights are long and lonely.
In vain I wait
Too long, too long.

In my room I sit alone.
Soon the light grows dimmer
The walls creep closer
And loneliness grips my soul.

I see you there, Martha
Your hand outstretched
Your beckoning smile
Your form divine.
Lighthearted I rise
To touch your hand
Martha, Oh Martha.....
Only memories and me.
June and September Martha
Are far apart
And now November
Grips my heart
No Martha, I do not ask
That you return
For in winter's dawn
My dreams with you will fly.

## Pills, Pearls, and Potions

*by Dr. Jane A. Passamonte*

Farewell Martha, farewell.
The snowy fields are calling.
Remember me as one
Who loved too late
But ever loved too well
So farewell, farewell.....

Pills, Pearls, and Potions — by Dr. Jane A. Passamonte

## YOU HAVE TOUCHED THE STARS

Come walk with me down Memory Lane,
And linger a while in silent bliss.
The green grass beckons,
The road is steeper... the heart beats faster,
The Nightingale beckons with song.
No more the carefree youth at play
Or climbing hills... or racing streams.
No furtive glance... no rendezvous.
Have no regrets... for youth is but the seed
For dreams of glory,
For worlds to conquer,
To flip the Light Fantastic,
And blow bubbles in the wind.
You reached for your star... it slipped your grasp.
Alas... it is a story told by many.
But lesser stars were yours,
To crown your many years.
You know them now by name,
They mimic you in fame.
Let not the memories of yesteryears
Becloud the dreams of tomorrow.
Go sing in the rain... and dance in the wind,
And laugh in the setting sun.
You have touched and loved,
And made this a better world.
Reach high for a handful of stars
And greet the Crimson Dawn.

Pills, Pearls, and Potions _____ by Dr. Jane A. Passamonte

## MEMORY LANE

Come walk with me down Memory Lane
And linger a while in silent bliss.
The green grass beckons
The road is steeper, the heart is weaker.
The nightingale welcomes with a song.
No more the carefree youth at play,
Or climbing hills, or racing streams.
No furtive glance, no rendezvous.
Have no regrets, for youth is but the seed
For dreams of glory, for worlds to conquer.
To flip the Light Fantastic
And blow bubbles in the wind.
A turn on Memory Lane
Shadows are heavy.
A crisp breeze creeps up your back
And curious owls ask "who-who-who"
I crouch along, lift faster a heavy foot.
The sky is lower than was at dawn.
I hear the song of a nightingale.
There is a light on the hillside.
A band of angels stood on the ledge
With a song of delight, they pointed a way.
Ah, sweet reverie, companion of a lonely heart.
Home of dreams of youth within us.
Of victories we won and some we lost.
Of ecstasies reached, of tears we shed.
Of mountains we climbed, and rocks we stumbled.
Now, patched and bandaged, and faltering step,
The hopes of tomorrows is what we get
And the dreams of yesteryear
Mingle with the hopes of many dawns to come.

Pills, Pearls, and Potions by Dr. Jane A. Passamonte

## A FRIEND IN DEED

Let me be your friend
And wipe the tear racing down your cheek.
Life deals some crippling blows...
And in that vast Desert of Intolerance
We dodge the rocks of Ignorance...
And bear our blows in pain.

Let me be your friend...
And sit beneath the arms of friendly oaks...
And let the scented breeze from fruited trees
Caress our saddened souls.

A fallen leaf does rest at our feet...
It flirted with the sun...
It danced in the wind...
And sang in the rain.
Like you and me, its life goes on...
It will shade a seedling.
Then sail on a babbling brook to distant shores...
To play its part... like you and me.

Pills, Pearls, and Potions      by Dr. Jane A. Passamonte

## WHAT FOOLS WE MORTALS BE

Dear Friend,

    I hope you are doing well and enjoying each day for whatever it may bring.  As I type this and look out the window, Nature is dressed in a filmy white gown made of snow flakes and fallen leaves and frozen flower petals.  A lazy but impulsive wind blows the gown and then whispers to the trees.  Angry leaves chase the wind, but to no avail.  And I, a helpless mortal, sit trapped and cold and wishing I could join them.  What fools we mortals be.  We cannot make a tree, nor a snow flake.  And we cannot run with the wind.  We are not allowed to touch the stars, we must only look at them.  Maybe if we were allowed to touch the stars, they would not be there for very long.

    God gave us a marvelous body.  It looks beautiful and works wonderfully.  But we mistreat it, misuse it, and often destroy it.  God also gave us a wonderful world, but we are making a mess of it.  God gave us freedom, and we are using it for the wrong purposes.  Yet 90 percent of the people all over the world are really wonderful.  As I traveled in different countries, I was impressed at how people were truly friendly and had the same basic Christian qualities whether they were Hindu or Moslem, etc.  The fault must lie in the automatic freedom in each person to be good or bad, to be friend or foe.  And a small number of people do not have the motivation or the strength or discipline to suppress the evil side and amplify the good side.

Pills, Pearls, and Potions

by Dr. Jane A. Passamonte

Here we are... you and I... sitting in the middle of a great technical, social and medical revolution. It is beyond the dreams of anyone living 50 to 75 years ago. And you and I can sit back and watch the whole show. What a privilege and opportunity. What would our parents think of what is going on now? And what will it be 50 years from now?

All these things give us a lot to think about. And a lot to be thankful for. Let us hope those who are dominated by evil instincts will not spoil it for the 5 billion good people in this world.

I must close this letter now for a good reason. I must go check some pecans I am roasting. Wish you were here. Do take good care of yourself. All the yesterdays are gone. We have only tomorrows left. May God be with you with every tomorrow.


Love,

Pills, Pearls, and Potions — by Dr. Jane A. Passamonte

## ME IN THE MIRROR

I looked in the mirror,
And what did I see... someone else
That looked like me.
I made a face... an awful face.
The mirror copied... oh, what a disgrace.
I laughed out loud... an eerie sound.
The mirror was silent... like a burial ground.
Oh, mirror of deceit...
Hide not the Ego in my soul.
Turn out the light...
Let the stars be my goal...
And let the Hand of Friendship...
Unlock a world of Smiles.


## WHERE ARE YOUR KEYS?

Man on his knees... outside... seems looking for something.
What are you looking for?, he was asked.
My house keys, he said.
Where did you have them last?, he was asked.
In the house, he said.
Then why not look for them in the house?
There is more light out here... it is too dark in the house... he said.

If you want to find yourself, you may have to look in your inner sanctions of yourself.

Pills, Pearls, and Potions — by Dr. Jane A. Passamonte

## YESTERDAY

Yesterday - I watched a golden leaf
Set sail on a babbling brook.
A nightingale sang it farewell
While a scented breeze
Spread the message thru the trees.

Oh! Yesterday - I dreamed
Of faraway shores
And knights in shining armor,
Of daring deeds and vanquished foes.

But gone is yesterday,
The hills are steeper,
The heart is weaker.
The honking geese are heading south,
October's chill creeps within.
Memories - Oh! sweet memories,
Of days of song and dance.

Let birthdays come
How blessed they are.
Fear not for tomorrow,
It is the hope of spring
That lifts the snowy burden of today.

Pills, Pearls, and Potions — by Dr. Jane A. Passamonte

Never count the yesteryears,
But praise the happy memories.
The victories you won,
The wars you lost.
The friends and foes,
The laughs and woes.
The dreams you chased,
The hopes you dared.

Weave them all into a crown
And wear it on a proud head,
For it is your day for many moons to come,
And the destiny of tomorrow stirs in your soul.

You have made this a better world
For having touched and loved.
Wear the crown - not for a day,
But till the sands of time run out.

Pills, Pearls, and Potions — by Dr. Jane A. Passamonte

## MEMORIES OF YESTERDAY - HOPES OF TOMORROW

Yesterday - I watched a golden leaf
Set sail on a babbling brook.
A nightingale sang it farewell
While a scented breeze
Spread the message thru the trees.

Oh! Yesterday - I dreamed
Of faraway shores
And knights in shining armor,
Of daring deeds and vanquished foes.

But gone is yesterday.
The hills are steeper,
The heart is weaker.
The honking geese are heading south,
October's chill creeps within.

Memories - Oh! sweet memories,
Of days of song and dance.

Let birthdays come!
How blessed they are.
Fear not for tomorrow,
It is the hope of spring
That lifts the snowy burden of today.

## Pills, Pearls, and Potions
*by Dr. Jane A. Passamonte*

Never count the yesteryears,
But praise the happy memories
And the hopes of tomorrows to come.
The victories you won,
The wars you lost.
The friends and foes,
The laughs and woes.
The dreams you chased,
The hopes you dared.

Weave them all into a crown
And wear it on a proud head.
Smile and wave to friend and foes
For they also share your joy and woes.

You have made this a better world
For having touched and loved.
Wear the crown! Not for a day,
But for as long as the stars are in your eyes.

Pills, Pearls, and Potions  by Dr. Jane A. Passamonte

## A TRUE FRIEND

Hold my hand, my friend.
Let not the fears and doubts of yesteryear
Becloud the sunshine of today.

Those sleepless nights,
Those anguished hours.
Those meals you missed,
Cause gripped by fright.
Those all have fled
Like mist before the rising sun.

The Green Valley of Hope lies before you.
There is no guarantee for tomorrow
And yesterday's has expired.
Today you are the chosen one,
To live and love and laugh.

To sing in the sunshine
And dance in the rain.
Lift your eyes to the heavens
And bless the earth at your feet.

Many are the hearts and minds
That you have touched and loved
And made for them a better world.

## Pills, Pearls, and Potions
*by Dr. Jane A. Passamonte*

When the storm winds blow
And fear and doubt chill you,
Listen for a voice within
To lead you thru the fog
Of fear and misunderstanding.

To a New Dawn, a new day,
The Green Valley of your Dreams.

Pills, Pearls, and Potions   by Dr. Jane A. Passamonte

## MANDY

Come home Mandy... come home;
Come home Mandy... come home;
The light is in the window...
The pot is on the stove.

Come home Mandy... come home;
You run from broken dreams
To the haunts of the Satanic Muse;
There to be tempted with Smokes
And Drugs... and Dire deeds.

Come home Mandy... come home;
Break the bonds enslaving you.
Turn back... quick Mandy...
Let not the burning gates engulf you.
Your youth has not vanished Mandy
Only passed to your alter ego.
Oh yes... you now recall... your child of love...
Who now does mimic you and often sheds your tears.
And casts her shadow on your floor.
Save those tears Mandy... and kick the Tempters to their fate.
Dump regrets with the thousand yesterdays.
Come home Mandy... come home...
Today we drink... and live... and love...
For tomorrow Mandy... tomorrow may never come.
Come home Mandy... hold my hand and walk down Memory Lane.
We will sing in the rain and dance in the midday sun.
The light is getting low Mandy...
Soon it will be dark...
Come home Mandy... come home.

Pills, Pearls, and Potions

by Dr. Jane A. Passamonte

## PARTING AT THE GATE

Shed no tears for the parting,
For they are ever present.
Free of pain and suffering,
And the shackles of us Mortals.
Free to laugh with you,
And dream your troubles away.
Let dark clouds roam at will,
Let blow the winds of chance.
The Guiding Spirit will be there,
And light the way for every tomorrow.

Pills, Pearls, and Potions — by Dr. Jane A. Passamonte

## REVERIE

Alone, with a touch of sadness in my soul,
I walk down memory lane.
Shadows lengthen, leaves dance in the wind,
And distant trees, wrapt in misty gowns
Gently bow to the passing breeze.
A flash of youth stirs within... climbing trees,
Or racing a butterfly... maybe a leaping frog...
Or a cool drink from a babbling brook,
And throw a rock at an unknown target.
Oh... to grasp a BIT OF PASSING YOUTH.
Sleepless nights bring thoughts of empty days...
Cold ingratitude has replaced the welcome smile...
Oh... to step back in time
To the green valleys... and the cool waters
And the promise of tomorrow...
To Flip the Light Fantastic of your dreams...
And touch the hearts of friend and foe.
But too far is the distant view...
Too low the setting sun...
Too slow the walk on rocky roads...
And the twins of ignorance and greed
Envelope you like a blinding sandstorm.
Let me greet the dawn atop the mountain...
And lift my face to the scented breeze.
I'll count the stars till Morpheus
Leads me thru adventurous dreams.
I've had my youth... my reckless fling,
My search for gold, my years of romance...
I've climbed the mountain... and laughed in the rain...
Now I'll just count tomorrows

## Pills, Pearls, and Potions
*by Dr. Jane A. Passamonte*

And dream of victories won... of battles lost...
I do not see the smiles or hear the calls
Of loved ones long departed,
But they cheer me on and show the way
And wait for me beyond the Gate.

Pills, Pearls, and Potions      by Dr. Jane A. Passamonte

## LET'S CLIMB THE MOUNTAIN TOGETHER

Come my friend, and leave behind
The pills and potions... the aches and pains...
The sleepless nights... the days of doubts and tears.
Youth flashed before you... those halcyon days.
Too soon the years crept in... and brought its friends...
You welcomed Wisdom, but cared not
For Aches and Pains... and Breaking Parts...
The distant scene was dimmed by Tears
For friends who parted at a glorious age...
For parts unknown... or the Pearly Gates.

Come... we will climb to the mountain top, just you and I...
The trails are steep and rocky... but flowers will nod,
And birds call out, and placid lakes, like jewels
Shimmer in the sun, while scented breezes lift our spirits.
We must keep climbing... tho hearts beat faster.
It's the climb that stirs our soul,
And reaches in the recesses of our mind...
For dreams of glory... of victories won...
Of mission accomplished, and soon with Nature be one.

Alas, my friend, we stand, breathless with ecstasy,
On the mountain top... just you and I,
A golden Sun sneaks below the horizon...
While God's creatures far below, slowly move
In the evening glow... each to his own... each to his destiny.
In the darkened night we will sleep
In nature's arms, with flora and fauna.
And the discordant calls of creatures of the night.

## Pills, Pearls, and Potions

*by Dr. Jane A. Passamonte*

In the dark of night... we wake to a world of wonder,
The sky is crowded with the brightest of stars,
Blinking and staring at us mortals.
In a trance, our mortal parts forgotten... and souls in ecstasy,
We watch the jeweled stars... so close... so part of us.
While a burnished copper Moon stands guard...
Lest some mortal dared to catch a Star...
A fitting Chaperone to a sky full of jewels.

We slept no more... and spoke not a word.
Dawn broke in like thunder...
And a blazing sun sent the darkness scurrying.
The stars in haste... left for outer space.

With hearts and souls lifted in fulfillment...
We had a glimpse of Heaven... in all its glory.
In silence we made our way
To a bandaid world below... and dreams of things to come.

Pills, Pearls, and Potions       by Dr. Jane A. Passamonte

## THE MOUNTAIN OF DESIRE

There it is my friend... the Mountain of Desire.
There are two mountains in our life,
The Mountain of Daily Living,
And the Mountain of Desire that crowns our daily life...
That lifts our heart and soul...
And brings us closer to our Creator...
And to better know ourselves.
We must climb the Mountain of Desire...
Climb to the very top... tho trails are steep
And legs get weak... The very top my friend.
And when darkness falls... we will sit and wait
And listen in the shadowy silence...
For soon a gentle breeze will whisper to dancing leaves...
The grand coming of a jeweled sky.
A multitude of glorious blinking stars
Fill the azure sky... and ecstasy and bliss
Envelope us... as we... awe struck... lift our souls...
And in spirit... move close to the stars.
Somewhere at some distant past...
We feel part of them... we try to understand when and where...
Yes, we are part of them... and feel it in our soul.
In silence we get a glimpse of Heaven...
And feel the spark of Divinity that stirs within us.

Pills, Pearls, and Potions

by Dr. Jane A. Passamonte

## THE GIFT OF TODAY - THE HOPE OF TOMORROW

Often, wrapt in reverie, we look at pictures of family members or friends... or we picture them in our thoughts. Many of them are on in years... or gone... it is a vivid reminder of yesteryear that embellishes our memories.

Today we live, and complacently accept each day. But it is more than that... Each day is a blessing and a gift... whether one is 20 or 80... the obituaries are testimony to that fact... Each day is a jewel on our invisible crown... Too often elder citizens are berated or belittled, not only by youth, but by family... and are relegated to minimal considerations... A small number are fortunate to have a loving and caring family... In years past we used to refer to them as old and did so respectfully. The Orientals still do that now... But Westerners, especially in the U.S.... lack reverence for old people... they are disposable like a plastic cup... Like a flower, born to bloom in the desert air, this wonderful treasure of wisdom, love, tolerance and understanding, is unsung... unloved and unseen... But tomorrow... that is the hope and the prayer... How wonderful to rise and greet the dawn... and give thanks for a night of rest. Each of us owns and is part of the life giving Sun and relishes its warmth... We must accept the sun as our life, for without the sun we would have no warmth... no food, no light, no anything... yet it is free... to you and me and to all creatures great and small... And look at the green grass that lovingly wraps itself around the world... adorned by flowers of radiant hues, and entertained by the song of birds and the humming of insects... And add to this the gentle breeze that lifts our spirits... scented by far away flowers and

Pills, Pearls, and Potions — by Dr. Jane A. Passamonte

cooled by mountain streams.  As you walk on the earth you are walking on sand and stones and bits of artifacts millions of years old... stepping on the footsteps of ancestors we never knew and animals that have been long gone... Clouds hover above us... maybe laden with rain... water that has been recycled since time began.

But soon the day comes to an end... and we are delighted by the orange glow of a setting Sun... like you and me it has made its run, and now prepares for the coming of a multitude of blinking Stars... a glorious spectacle, chaperoned by a prim Moon... Like you and me, the world prepares for a new tomorrow...  it is all free, for you and me.

Pills, Pearls, and Potions — by Dr. Jane A. Passamonte

## GEREN

I come to you Thalia... Muse of Song,
Goddess of friendship,
Not for myself... but for my good friend, Geren.
Write a song, and tell the world of his dedication
No work too great... no task too small... no hour too long.
And in a stirring chord;
With flourishing notes;
Tell of his love for his fellowman.

Sometimes rapt in thought,
Harsh realities cloud the wishful dreams,
And cold winds of Reason...
Blow out the candle of Desire.
Write a song... a light fantastic tune;
Let the words be warm... and bursting as with Spring.
Of things desired... of dreams untold.
Of cherished love... and hopes that soon unfold.


Let there be no discordant note... no sadness in the lyrics.
Let the moonbeams pierce the shadows in my friend's mind.
The sorrow in his heart... the loneliness in his soul.

And above all Thalia... open the window of understanding.
No saddened glance... no fractured Cymbals.
Let the music fill the air,
Let every note strike a smile...
Every word bring happiness.

This I ask Thalia, for my friend Geren...
Farewell Thalia... Muse of song... Goddess of friendship...
Farewell.

Pills, Pearls, and Potions

by Dr. Jane A. Passamonte

## BIRTHDAY

A birthday is a time to remember not only the memories of the past year... but of all the years since you were born. Then all the challenges, hopes and dreams of the years ahead. It is a time to be grateful for all the blessings... that like the gentle rain from Heaven, have fallen on you and yours. It is a time to look around to the many wonderful things in scientific, medical, social and economic advances we are enjoying today... that we did not have many years ago... and to think of what it will be in the near future. It is a time to appreciate the many gifts we enjoy of freedom, a green and growing environment... the warm sun and the cooling breezes... and abundance of food, clean water, clean air and fertile land. Surely we must protect ourselves from the few who desecrate these free gifts... this will be an ever challenge. Let us strive in making this a better world, for we are part of a whole universe, and we rise or fall together. On one's birthday, millions of others will also have a birthday, and many will be lonely, or hungry or in pain... so while we rejoice on our birthday, let us wish in our hearts we could lift the spirits and bring a smile to the forlorn and forgotten.

Listen... and in the deep recesses of your mind you will hear the silent calls of Love and Happy Birthday from mountain to mountain and from sea to sea...

## TO J. B.

Grab the rails J. B.————————— Hold tight,
Stormy winds swirl and sway us,
Thru the uncertain sea of life.

Fickle waves reach out their gaping jaws,
While fat swells carry us aloft,
It's a game they play, like the game of life.

Oh, that God would lend me a touch of Eloquence,
To match the coming Dawn,
There is a bright tomorrow,
Thru the darkness and the storm.

Hold tight to the rails,
They were put there for you and me.
For storms do come - J. B.
But also comes the promise of tomorrow.

Flip the light fantastic,
Dance with the whirling winds,
And taunt the angry seas.

Laugh, and let the world laugh with you,
Jump and cheer with joy.
Grab a handful of stars, and laughingly - J. B.,
Thrust them in the angry sea.

Just for the fun of it - J. B.
Just for the fun of it.

Pills, Pearls, and Potions

by Dr. Jane A. Passamonte

## EARTH ANGELS

All of us have one or more problems to contend with... They are part of our life and living... and in many cases the price we pay for added blessings of longevity, family, wisdom and understanding... The more senior years we add to our lives is evidence that it is for a purpose and a mission. A lot has been said about Angels... Some Angels, without wings, or Earth Angels, are all around us... When needed, these Angels are touched or led in some mysterious way, to help some deserving Mortal... The one who is being helped may wonder why this stranger or friend or relative is being so helpful... But at the same time both the giver and the receiver of help, feels an inner lift of Spirit and well-being... there is a rhapsody of the Soul they enjoy but cannot understand... How do I know all this?... Because I have been a receiver many a time and a giver as well. And I know many others who have done the same... Like the sun and the wind and the rain... Earth Angels play their part. They help another Mortal, be it in a physical, emotional, mental or even spiritual. Earth Angels understand and love their fellow Mortals. Often the task is long and difficult... often just a warm loving touch and a smile... or a sign that someone cares. The reward is equally great and elating to the giver and the receiver... How do you receive this angelic help?... You must first examine yourself, your talents and your abilities. You must have done all you can to help yourself... using all your physical, emotional and natural abilities... When you have exhausted all your earthly resources, you then look upward for Divine guidance and Faith... That is from where Earth Angels get their orders and directions... Oh, yes... Ask anyone who has been in a real crisis. Someone who could not go back... and did not know

Pills, Pearls, and Potions — by Dr. Jane A. Passamonte

what was ahead... maybe only a heart beat from the dark beyond.  Earth Angels can be of any age.  So can be the receiver of their help.  The body may be real young or real old... but the Spirit, the moving force within our clay exterior, is ever the same.  We have a lot within us to make us great, wise and strong... but we must find out what we have... and honestly know our potential and ourselves for what we are and then do our best...  The Earth Angels will take care of the rest... cause they are guided by the Divine Spirit that guides us all... But help is for those with faith and trust in themselves and the Divine Spirit and have exhausted all their mortal assets.  As for the heavenly winged Angels, that is another great story.
I will let you tell me about them.

Pills, Pearls, and Potions                                    by Dr. Jane A. Passamonte

## LOOK INWARD AND UPWARD

When one is ill... often seriously... they are physically, emotionally and spiritually disturbed. There is pain, anger, anxiety, fear... The family also suffers... and to varying degrees, the friends, neighbors and fellow workers and to a less extent society in general... Each one of us is part of a larger whole... When one hurts, or falls, or cries in pain, the ripple of our tragedy goes far and wide. Many sick people have exhausted the medical and other means of curing... They have reached the end of the road... and now view the dark, deep, chasm of the unknown... Surely it is a desperate moment... Those who have been there are rarely able to convince those who have not... of the agony, desperation and fear... They are only a heart beat between their past memories and the dark uncertain beyond... There is no turning back.

Now one must look inward and upward... for there lies the answer... the strength and understanding of one's self... the faith and hope of a greater Spirit that gave us our beginning and will now direct our future.

Pills, Pearls, and Potions     by Dr. Jane A. Passamonte

## A LUMP OF CLAY

You and I, my friend... are but a lump of clay;
Shaped and sharpened by a hand Divine...
And gifted with a Soul.
Full many a time, the clay that binds...
Will chip or crack... or fail to hold.
Full many a tear will cloud the distant view.
But we must move on... and play our part.
We sing our song... tho with saddened heart.
We dance in the rain... and laugh in the wind.
'Tis not the clay that counts, but the goal ahead...
And the soul within.

The flute is but a piece of wood...
Like you and I, my friend.
It stirs no thoughts... makes no sounds.
But listen with joy... when someone... like you and I...
Mortals as we be... do blow our Spirit...
Thru the fragmented tree.

There is a part we all must play...
To blow the flute and summon the Angels.
To walk the long and lonely road...
Greeted by songs of birds... and flowers nodding in the breeze...
Or aiding a weary traveler... maybe wiping a few tears.
...'Tis not the feet of clay... that measures the miles...
But the Spirit within us...
That spreads the Smiles.

Pills, Pearls, and Potions — by Dr. Jane A. Passamonte

## THE SECRET OF RAD BELSEN

Rad Belsen faced a real crisis in his life... his future and his health were involved... his past cast a certain shadow on his present and future. He had tried cover ups, lies, bribes and even thought of suicide. He asked advice from friends at the bars and even a doctor friend. On a plane trip, he sat with an elderly and friendly man with whom he soon started a casual conversation. Soon it led to Rad's problems... and an exchange of names followed. Rad's seat mate was Professor Klingman, who headed the social counseling department at the medical school. Rad unloaded all his present and past to this wonderful man who listened with warmth and understanding. Then Rad asked, "What can I do?" Professor Klingman asked, "Can you be real honest with yourself? I mean real honest. Then confess to yourself the evils you have done to others and to yourself, the sadness and hurts you have caused. Examine your relation with yourself, your family and your God. What have you done to yourself and to family and friends that was rewarding to you, that gave you a lift, or a smile, or a happy feeling? You have looked everywhere for advice in your crisis. You will find the answer when you search your soul and look up to God. The answer is within you and you alone."

Pills, Pearls, and Potions — by Dr. Jane A. Passamonte

Dr. Klingman offers this incident to his Medical School class for discussion.

I must go back to the banks of the Ahmalor... for there my inner Spirit... the longing in my mind has its roots. In the luxury of my home, often I sit, comfortable and relaxed, but wrapt in reverie, of my days on the banks of the Ahmalor. With my Dad we go fishing. With great pride I help him reel in the fish... or unsnag the line... or toss a few rocks into a swirling pool. A low branch on a towering oak is a challenge to climb... and catching a frog makes me a hero for the day.

My reverie is broken by an urgent call from a patient, for I am now Dr. Greg Brandon... and I am glad to be on call and help my patients. Often sleep is overpowered and displaced by the Spirit within. My mind goes back to the Ahmalor... to happy and careless days. There were games, picnics, flirtations, and pride in achievements. There was the lavish love and attention of a loving mom and dad... and yes, friends galore and romping retreats by the Ahmalor... High school years brought new biological changes and a different perspective of girls. This increased and carried on into college. That is where I met Amy. I met and dated several fine girls in college, but Amy was different. I felt at ease with her, with an inner feeling that she was part of me... an important part that made me whole and happy. When we were together, I felt that we were sufficient unto ourselves and that nothing else mattered. Fancy cars, money, material possessions did not matter, only that we be together, face each day, each year, for what it was and face ourselves for what we were. I was able to look into myself for what I was... and what I was not... to make the best of what I was and face the future for whatever

## Pills, Pearls, and Potions

*by Dr. Jane A. Passamonte*

it brought... using all my talents while suppressing or improving all my weak points. With this in mind, and dreaming of a great future, I asked Amy to marry me. She waited a week to give me the answer... She said she was not sure... she had to think more about it. Ten days later she gave me a positive NO. She would not tell me why and refused all future dates and calls. I went on to finish Med school a long way from Ahmalor, and further away to start my medical practice...

Recently I got a letter from Amy... it read;
Dear Greg, I really do not know how to start or finish this letter. My years have been traumatic and I find myself lonely and forsaken. I must tell you that I always loved you and you alone... When I was with you I felt I was in a heavenly world... a world I wished to share with you... a world in which there would be no sad regrets... no tears... no dark clouds of doubt... or fears... or misunderstanding. I could not imagine living without you. Then along came Ben... a big handsome and popular football player. In my naive thinking, I felt elated by his attention... and I was swept off my feet and sensible thinking. We were married. He became most unfaithful and neglectful of me and after three years, left me. Caught in a vacuum of despair and loneliness, I found some consolation and comfort with George H., 7 years older than me and full of promises and lies. His promises blinded me into marriage. He had money to support me well, but he was alcoholic, very abusive, and often violent to me. The misery and unhappiness of the first marriage, plus the violence and abuse of George, led to severe inner misery, depression and despair. Medical treatment was of no value and even the doctor advised that I divorce George for my health. I did... but my health continued to decline. Soon I was told I had colon

## Pills, Pearls, and Potions
*by Dr. Jane A. Passamonte*

cancer that had spread. My time now is limited... I spend my days and my sleepless nights with thoughts of you and what you meant to me. Silently and alone, I cry for you... and wish for the days gone by when you held me in your arms. I am running out of time and tears, but my love for you is ever stronger... I see you everywhere and often hear your voice. I will not say Goodbye, Greg... for I know we will meet in another world, and again return to the banks of the Ahmalor.

Dr. Klingman's advice to students...
Examine your inner selves... your talents, courage and confidence... your weaknesses, your strengths and motivations. Your future health and happiness depends on how well you use your inner wealth. This is your lifetime asset and strength... It cannot be stolen, lost or broken... It will grow with you, and you can do anything you want within your inner talents, courage, confidence and understanding. You cannot put a money value on it. The value of money is only what you make it within your talents. Of itself it has no value. But the value of your inner spirit... your understanding... your love of your fellowman, your sharing of your self and your talents... that is your greatest wealth and happiness. An Arab merchant was once asked by a customer what was a good rug for him... The merchant told him to sit by a pile of rugs and flip them one at a time. Then the merchant said, "When you come to the one that makes you feel good inside, that is your rug." Dr. Klingman says, "This you can apply to anything you want... from rugs to cars... to shoes, etc... try it."
Dr. Klingman asks, "What about Amy's fading health? And is Greg caught in the same emotional and heartbreaking storm, facing the same fate?" It has been shown that when a

## Pills, Pearls, and Potions
*by Dr. Jane A. Passamonte*

person faces a severe crisis with tension, fear, despair, disappointment, disgrace, etc., the body functions that lead to healthy living are either suppressed or destroyed. There is a decreased or absent support for the good cells and organs to function. This gives the bad viruses and bacteria an opportunity to overcome the good cells, and multiply faster than normal cells, and soon develop cancers and tumors, clots and various diseases. The exhausted body is unable to adequately grow and defend itself. It's immunity is suppressed or destroyed. There is a deep desire for the days of youth... the simple values... the extended family... the playground of imagination... fantasy... aspiration... the security of home and a loving and doting family and friends.

The memory is bonded in the heart and brain, and now is a most valuable asset. It is what you hang on to for dear life, in a tornado or fearsome and dire events. Money and materialism have no value. You are between the beginning and the end. You quickly scan the events of the past... the victories and the defeats... The future is misty and uncertain... How comforting to turn to the Spirit above for help... You are alone with your Maker... And you make new promises to yourself and to your God... Now we find out that we live and laugh or cry by the truths and values within us... By what we give of ourselves in love, wisdom and understanding and tolerance... Therein lies the security and wealth of the future... the health of our mind and body... We can measure how far we have gone, not by the miles... but by the Smiles we have left behind.

Your past has the combination that will unlock and shape the future. It is all yours for what you make it... You can go back to the banks of the Ahmalor or be lost in the Forest of frustration, fears and regrets.

Pills, Pearls, and Potions — by Dr. Jane A. Passamonte

## TRUE LOVE

Oh how I wish my friend
I could crown your head
With pearls from the ancient sea...
But then I would miss the depth of Ecstasy
Like the friendship between you and me.
There is no emerald... green and glorious
No diamond... glowing and bright...
That could fill my soul
And lift my spirits
Like the friendship from your heart
And the lovelight from the stars in your eyes.
The days may be long and lilting
The nights long and lonely.
You may be near or far...
You still do fill my heart and soul.
While silent words my spirit does speak
And my mind knows well and speaks soothingly
And smiles... and laughs and sings in rhapsody
And I know that all is well... my friend
That all is well...
In the silence of our souls.

Pills, Pearls, and Potions     by Dr. Jane A. Passamonte

## STORMY SKIES

When matrimonial skies are stormy
And you've lost your faith in yourself
Read a few pages
Then close your eyes.
Look in the mirror... just a little longer
When you open your eyes
What a relief... the skies are clearer
A smile on your face...
What a wonderful worldlook for some to embrace.
How great to be alive
Tell someone... I love you.

Pills, Pearls, and Potions — by Dr. Jane A. Passamonte

## HIM

Alone... all alone... I stood atop the Mt. of Desire...
A weathered pine bowed to a whistling wind
And darkening clouds crowded the sky.
My arm reached out... searching for someone
To curb the emptiness within me...
My eyes searched the sky.
I hoped for a voice, a touch, a guiding light
Then a whisper came from within my soul
Like a light from the dark caverns of my mind...
"You are not alone My child...
For within you... the strength of past souls
Are ever leading you... and silent thoughts
Direct you in deeds present and past
And light the way, the mind and the inner self.
You are the essence of thousands of souls
The child of many angels around you.
Look within you and listen to the silent voice of the past.
The spark of Divinity is ever within you...
You are not alone.

Pills, Pearls, and Potions — by Dr. Jane A. Passamonte

## TRUE FRIEND

Hello, my friend.
I have never met you and do not know you...
And you do not know me.
We are two people in the billions in this world.

How many people have you and I walked by,
Said maybe a "Hello" or "How are you" and never met again.

Do you have a real friend? I do not.
Sure, we have a lot of acquaintances, many we call friends
And many we meet to eat and drink... have social hour
Or night... then you go to your residence and realize you
Were not with a true friend. Only a transient moment in
A whirling wind, with good intentions, but fragile fabric,
Fleeting moments... promised to meet again and soon forget
Each other.

Even when it could be husband and wife, or there is a physical,
Social or financial tie that did not meet the test of time.

You may consider true friends members of a club, Sunday
School, church, neighbor or workplace.
Yet, when the time comes to prove it... only a very few
Are true friends, the rest are just convenient friends,
Serving a momentary purpose.
Some fill in the gap... as a school teacher, spouse or
School pal. Some like to feel important with many of
The actions of a friend.

## Pills, Pearls, and Potions
*by Dr. Jane A. Passamonte*

When the need comes to act as a friend, they completely
Fail the real action of a true friend. They can find
More excuses and apologies for failing to be the friend
They made you think they were.
And they failed to be the friend you wanted them to be
And needed now.

Climb the highest mountain... catch the falling star.
Is a true friend much afar?
Dr. Klingman of the Institute of Human Relations
Says "Maybe not."
A true friend can tell when you are sad and lonely.
There may be many people around you that come and go.
You converse and laugh with them.

They may bring gifts and sporadic hugs...
But, inside your heart and soul, you are lonely.
You need to light the dark cavern in your soul and mind.
And no one has the spark you wish for... you wish for that
Special touch or smile or the hug of understanding.

How many a smile deep in as many hearts is wasted on the
Vast desert of humans.
They are misdirected and lost in the whirling wind of
Human frailty.

Many a time, a lonely and sad soul wishes for a kind
Touch or kind word to light the spark in their soul...
To brighten the stars in his eyes...
To lift the burdens of life.

**Pills, Pearls, and Potions** — by Dr. Jane A. Passamonte

What a gift is a good hug, when least expected,
When four walls seem to bury your dreams and
Embrace you in darkness.

A real friend can open the door to a heaven of love.
A real friend can feel your need.
A great gift is a real friend.

Take along your smile, your touch, a simple wildflower
And take a walk in the park or in the woods or just
Some silent moments together.

Real friends understand so much, just with silent
Conversation.  So much is said and understood
In the silent conversations of the soul between
Real friends.

Pills, Pearls, and Potions

by Dr. Jane A. Passamonte

## LIFE'S DRAMA

You and I, Joe... were born a bundle of chemistry
Wrapped in a baby blue coat
And supplied with a loud pair of lungs.
To let everyone know... "Here we are."
We blew our own horn and gathered a crowd.
As we grew, the doctor knew a lot about our chemistry.
We swallowed a lot of nasty medicine, more chemistry...
Got lots of shots and frequent poking by Dr. Brown.

Then, we started school. Plenty of nice kids, but also
A bunch of bullies... some real nasty.
We thought then that school was a waste of time.
Even now, who cares about arithmetic and geography.
But on we went for twelve years.
But as you said, "There was some good."

To get a job there was the same old questions...
"Do you have a high school diploma?"
No diploma... no job... no girlfriend.
The years passed, we got wise.

Now it's rent, kids, jobs... some aches and pains...
And sixty years grinning at you.
Grandkids all over... and no job a threat.

Soon forced on welfare. Good times are over.
Retirement homes... what a poor choice.
Dumped, no teeth, no hair... arthritis is your pal.

We have lived the whole drama.
We wait for the call... the Angel Gabriel to open the gate.

Pills, Pearls, and Potions — by Dr. Jane A. Passamonte

## YOU AND ME... JOE

Come, Joe... Let's go find another world. We could be great.
We have done so much. We fly faster than birds. We can
Talk around the world. We walk on the moon and give it a
Whirl. We write millions of words on barely a chip...
And we visit our friends, each miles away. The voice and a
Picture, a telephone marvel are here to stay. Who would
Think it would ever be. We cure ancient ills, and swap
Organs with ease. We operate on babies unborn. With scopes
Supreme we can see things unseen and use sound to see
Things hidden.

This is all great, Joe... just great... but, not for us humans,
You and I. All over this world, for one or more reasons,
Humans are slaughtered... yes, Joe. Babies and mothers,
Young and old, slaughtered for reasons never told, and egos
Ever present, built bigger than ever. While angels of evil
Fill the unreasonably clouded air. What happened to brotherly
Love? Gone is the sacred home. Gone is the ancient trust
And the jails are filled.

But, loneliness darkens the home.
Too soon, we trust our elders
Who nursed us with love and care... where love is gone, care
Is forsaken. And who knows where and when the laws were
Broken.

## Pills, Pearls, and Potions

*by Dr. Jane A. Passamonte*

Come, Joe... Let's find another world.  Stay close, Joe...
It's just you and me.  What good is a transplanted liver or
Even another heart?  I would rather find a friend to share
Our smiles and understanding.  To tolerate and forgive
Some dark moment of dissent, then fly the skies to nowhere.
Or even praise the shallow glory of victories never won.

Let's find some friends, Joe... and cleanse the evil from our
Souls.  Let's shake hands and trade hearty laughs and smiles...
Another world is hard to find.  Let's reshape the one we've got
Just you and I, Joe... and the angels above.